M O V I N G   W A T E R

An Artist's Reflections on Fly Fishing, Friendship and Family

Dave Hall

Blaine Creek Press
MovingWater.org

Requests for permission to make copies of any part of the work should be sent to: MovingWater.org.

ISBN: 978-0-692-14734-4

Printed in the United States of America.

Book design by Jim Hayes, Ha! Yes! Design, Salt Lake City.
Osprey sketches by Jim Hayes, from photos by Graham Owen.
Thanks to Rick Bass for the "quill pen scratching" reference in the sporting journal story.
Thanks also to Steve Hausknecht for permission to use the cover painting *Dawn on the North Fork*.

F O R E W O R D

I have spent much of my life thigh deep in moving water.

Two grandfathers led me to fishing, and I was fortunate to have lived in rural New England where the absence of roads and fences nourished a young boy's passion for finding fish.

Family art hung in our home — my father, a grandmother, a great, great grandfather. These gifted artists gave me permission, I suppose, to do what I do. And they've encouraged me in ways mysterious.

Along the way, a handful of friends have spent countless days in various countries longing for trout to rise and for bonefish to tail in the sweep of tropical tides.

Our passions give birth to our stories. And the characters in our best stories are those we care most about.

We are our stories…

Last Chance, Idaho

August, 2018

In 1956 when I was seven my grandfather gave me a fiberglass rod, a Medalist reel, a box of flies and this advice: "You fish with a rod, not a pole." The rest, as they say, is history.

Morning On The North Fork

And my grandfather's grandfather, the sporting artist Thomas Henry Snow, was an angler and bird hunter. His leatherbound journal, with 106 entries from April 22, 1856 to December 12, 1873, has been entrusted to me.

You can almost hear the quill pen scratching the paper in the evening light in his Boston home, not far from the marshes he loved.

My grandfather, foreground. *His* grandfather,
the sporting artist Thomas Henry Snow, looks on.
Medford, Massachusetts, 1906

Brook Trout, Thomas Henry Snow, 1871

As a kid in New England I discovered topo maps. It took me no time to learn that the thinner the black lines, the more interest they held for me. And the thin blue lines—moving water!—were the most interesting of all. These brooks, as we called them, wandered through dense green woodlands and fields with ancient oaks. And their beauty too was that they were off the state's trout stocking schedule, so no one fished them. On an April morning—the day of my first high school baseball game—I rose early and fished alone a secret farm pond and caught a trophy native brookie on a hand-tied Mickey Finn streamer. On the path home I met my Dad at a creek crossing and he asked "How'd you do?" I reached in the back of my mail order Bean vest and showed him.

The Lamar Valley

A mile from my home there was a spring pond in the woods. No one knew about it we were sure. We caught brookies painted in fall's rich colors. I'd take my spaniel Zerk and he'd sit beside me as I cast — shaking, especially with a hookup.

One day he disappeared to the far shore. My calls of *Zerk! Come!* were ignored. He wagged back with a mallard in his mouth. I freed her and she exploded through the trees, feathers falling with the maple leaves.

Summer, 1982: Fishing The Ranch in Last Chance, a fly box floated down to me. I returned it to the owner upstream. He turned out to be a poet from New York and Key West. Later that morning he introduced me to Neal from Steamboat, who introduced me the next day to Frank from Denver, who introduced me the following summer to Tobey from Vermont and Rob from Cape Cod. A quick finger count tells me that since then we've fly fished together in ten countries. Chance encounters...

Thurman Creek, Harriman Ranch

Fishing the Henry's Fork, I found a nice rainbow sipping against the bank. It had been a tough weekend—few fish—so I rode my bike fast back to the bunkhouse and found Schmidt. Get your rod I said. We jumped on the bike the two of us—him on the seat and me peddling— and we rode like maniacs the mile back to the fish. Schmidt took one cast and nailed him, just like that.

The Henry's Fork And Sawtell

DAVE HALL

Years ago I was fishing with a friend, a novice fly fisherman but a world-class climber. At lunch leaning against a boulder he said "You know, fly fishing is just like climbing. There's all kinds of equipment, you go to the most beautiful places in the world, you do it with your very best friends, and everyone's obsessed."

Snow In The Hills

A number of springs ago I was at the house alone on Blaine Creek, fighting a bout of the blues. Late morning when the mayflies were dancing above the creek, I grabbed my rod and dropped off the bench. In minutes I had a ten-inch brown in hand. I snapped its neck, getting it over quick like I was taught as a kid. Then, sitting on the bank among the willows watching the warblers in from the south, I began to cry. When that was over, I climbed the hill to the house and cooked the trout in lemon and butter only and ate it with a side of pasta with fresh Parmesan and pepper and a watercress garnish from the creek—a meal you can't buy anywhere.

Indian Creek Overlook

Floating the Madison Varney to Eight Mile with Jules, we got caught in a brutal storm. We beat it to shore and flipped the Avon raft over us. We talked and laughed, played cribbage and drank rum until the weather passed.

The Yellowstone River Headwaters

I was thinking it doesn't get much better:
It's June, and Frank and I are skipping
across the Idaho potato fields, heading to
the Park to fish. It's first light, the windows
are down, Becky's pregnant with Sarah.
We've got the Stones cranked up and we're
laughing and singing *Dead Flowers* loud.
Wild Horses works, too.

East Across The Madison Valley

The thing about fishing in Grizzly Country is this: You've got your bear spray close but there's still a chance (small) you'll get eaten.

Wilderness…

Add a bull moose, river otters, wolf tracks on the gravel meanders, ospreys, eagles, ocher grasses to your chest, and silence but for the wind across the meadow, and you realize that this place has changed little since Thomas Henry Snow was hunting ducks on Boston's Back Bay marshes before the Civil War.

Moving Water

Years ago a mid-life crisis led to a year-long family sojourn in a one-dock Bahamian village. Several times a week I'd ride my old bike, fly rod across the handlebars, through town past the Colonial cottages and down the coral path to greet the flood tide on the bonefish flats—a grown man loving being 12 again.

And a couple days a week I'd sneak away in my 30-horse Whaler, hugging the coast twenty minutes into a soft Bahamian breeze—past the osprey nest, through the mangroves and arriving just as the tide turns, then waiting…waiting…for the shimmering bonefish tails.

Briland

A piece of my heart rarely wanders from moving water, thanks to the convergence of family and friends and the magic of mayfly hatches.

The Rise

Dawn On The Henry's Fork

The year Tobey died we took him for a final visit to his beloved New Zealand, staying at the home he built in Murchison at the confluence of the Mangles and the Blackwater. He wanted to float and fish the old rivers, so we brought inflatable kayaks, and Neal carried him where the wheelchair couldn't. One morning Tobey and I were driving alone up the Buller Valley heading to the Matakitaki to meet the others. The views were beautiful, and I stopped for photos. Back in the car, after a few minutes in silence, Tobey said "You know, we need to do more of that." I said "What, Tob?" He said "We need to slow down. We're always trying to get to the next river."

Buller Valley

Not long after that trip four families gathered for three days in the Yellowstone backcountry. We sang *Amazing Grace* at the confluence of two wild rivers. And we returned Tobey to the moving water he loved.

Day's End

His daughter, ten at the time, said her Dad would return as a bird. We agreed he would be an osprey. Now, when we see the great fish hawk on the Henry's Fork in Idaho or above a Montana spring creek or hunting the tropical flats, we whisper, *Tobey, Tobey, Tobey...*

Dawn

If you're lucky, there are places you go back to. Memories. Cribbage on the bank. Talks in the tent with Frank. Elk steaks by Neal. Garden pesto one night. A trip with Rob and a big rainbow that takes an ant, freaks out, and does a tarpon imitation, landing right on the bank. Tobey's ashes are a few meanders downstream.

Our trips become our stories and our stories become our dreams.

In one of my favorite dreams, there's an angler on the far bank, thigh deep in moving water, tough to see in the dawn's half light.

He — or she — is waiting for a trout to rise.

In this dream there is an osprey.

And the osprey is luffing silently skyward, up past the conifers and through the mist and fog of a Henry's Fork morning.

I hope…

I hope that *your* stories become *your* dreams.

www.ingramcontent.com/pod-product-compliance
Lightning Source LLC
Chambersburg PA
CBHW040824300326
41914CB00074B/1674/J